Ordering Information:
Quantity sales. Special discounts are available on quantity purchases by corporations, associations, and others. For details, contact the author at the email address above.

Printed in the United States of America

BELIEVE IN YOURSELF

Believe in yourself and in your dream
Though impossible things may seem

Someday somehow you'll get through
to the goal you have in view

Mountains falls and seas divide
before the one who in his stride

Takes the hard road day by day
Sleeping obstacles away

Believe in yourself and in your plan
Say not - I can't - but yes I can

The prizes of life will fail to win
Because we doubt the power within

~ Author Unknown
~ With love,
Connie Omari LPC NCC

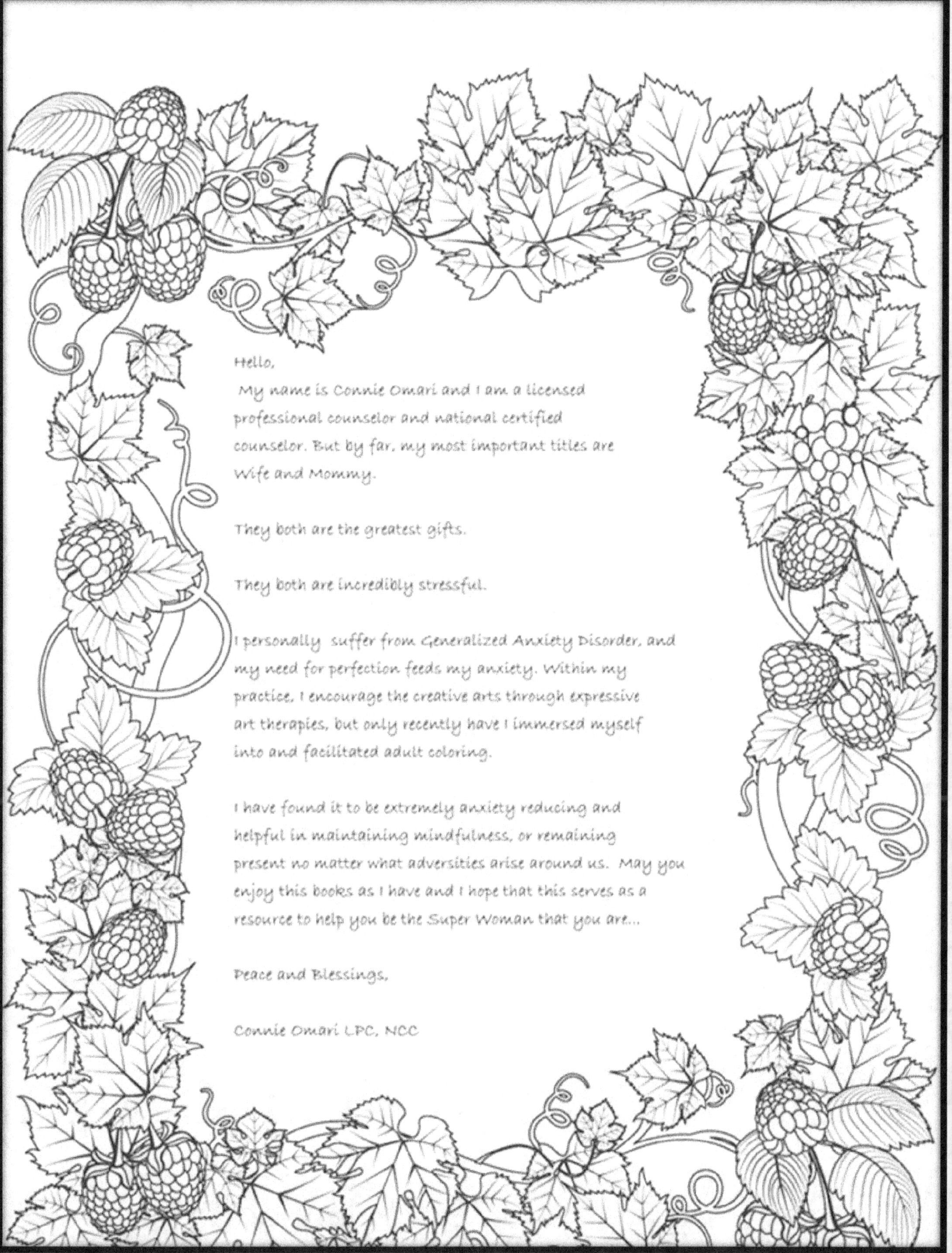

Hello,

My name is Connie Omari and I am a licensed professional counselor and national certified counselor. But by far, my most important titles are Wife and Mommy.

They both are the greatest gifts.

They both are incredibly stressful.

I personally suffer from Generalized Anxiety Disorder, and my need for perfection feeds my anxiety. Within my practice, I encourage the creative arts through expressive art therapies, but only recently have I immersed myself into and facilitated adult coloring.

I have found it to be extremely anxiety reducing and helpful in maintaining mindfulness, or remaining present no matter what adversities arise around us. May you enjoy this books as I have and I hope that this serves as a resource to help you be the Super Woman that you are...

Peace and Blessings,

Connie Omari LPC, NCC

She Believed She Could
So She Did...

Don't let yesterday take up too much of your today...

Some Birds are Not Meant
to be Caged

No Garden Truly Blooms
until Butterflies
have Danced
Upon it.

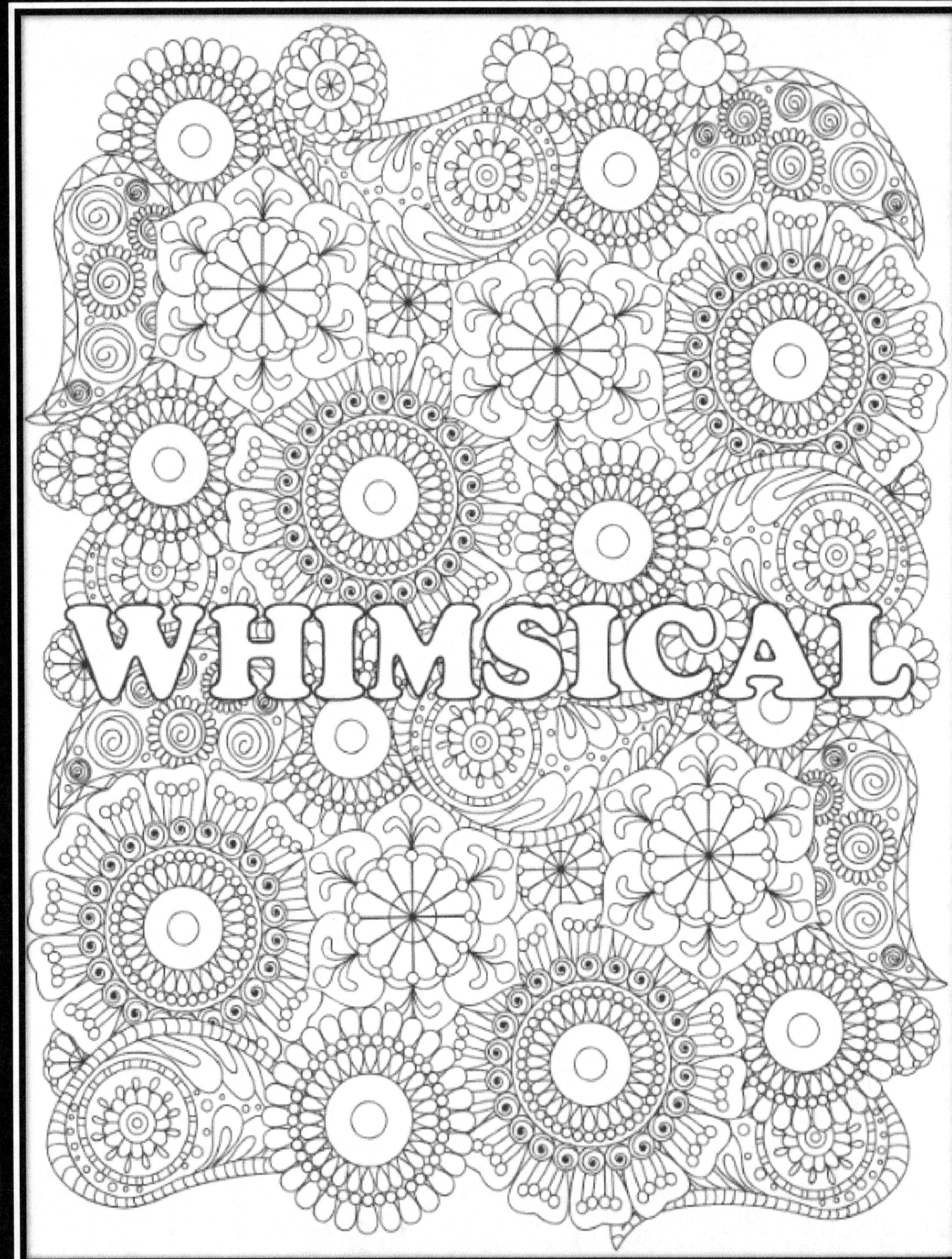

WHIMSICAL

TRUE BEAUTY

There's Always a
Second Chance

Never Too Late
to Change.

A WOMAN is the FULL CIRCLE.
Within Her is the Power to Create,
Nurture and Transform.

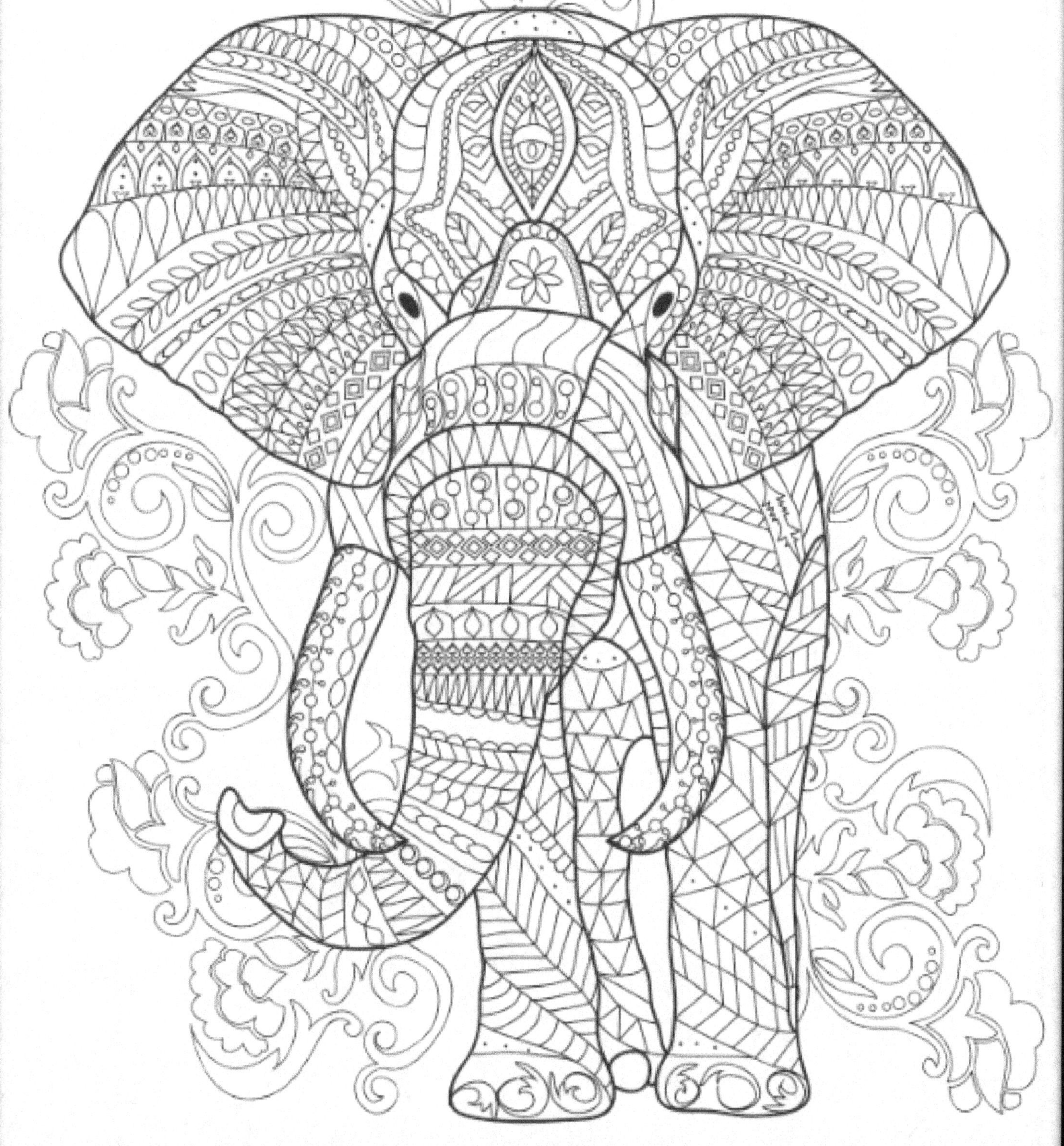All Good Things are
Wild and Free

BELIEVE

Be a Flamingo. Stay Balanced.
Stand by your Flock,
And Always be Fabulous!

You do have a Story Inside You;
it Lies Articulate and Waiting to be
Written Behind Your Silence and Your Suffering.

Life is a Series of waves
to be Embraced
and Overcome

No One Can Make You
Feel Inferior
Without Your Consent.

You prepare a table before me
in the presence of my enemies.
You anoint my head with oil.
My cup runs over.
Psalm 23:5

I am fearfully
and
wonderfully made
Psalm 139:14

Courage is Like a Muscle.
We Strengthen it by Use

PERSEVERANCE

Give and Receive
GRACE

Give Birth to something
Greater than yourself ...

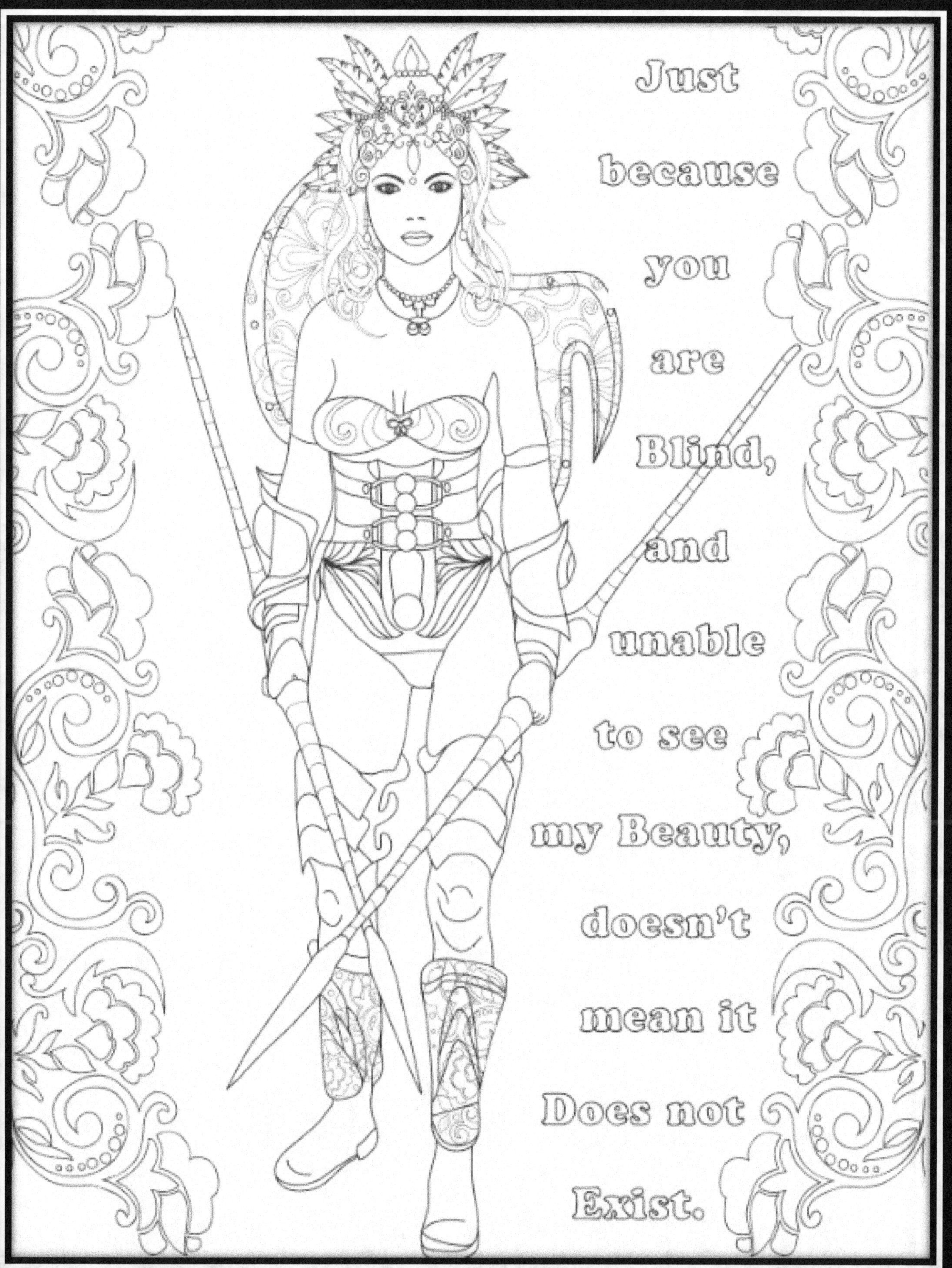
Just
because
you
are
Blind,
and
unable
to see
my Beauty,
doesn't
mean it
Does not
Exist.

FAITH

A Girl Should be
Two Things:
Who and What
She Wants

Vulnerability
is
Strength

See the birds
of the sky,
that they
don't sow,
neither do they reap,
nor gather into barns.
Your heavenly Father feeds them.
Aren't you of much more value than they?
Matthew 6: 26

I am a Princess Warrior

Think like a Queen...
A Queen is not Afraid to Fail.
Failure is Another Stepping Stone
to Greatness.

Be Full of Wonder

HOPE

Failure
is not
an option

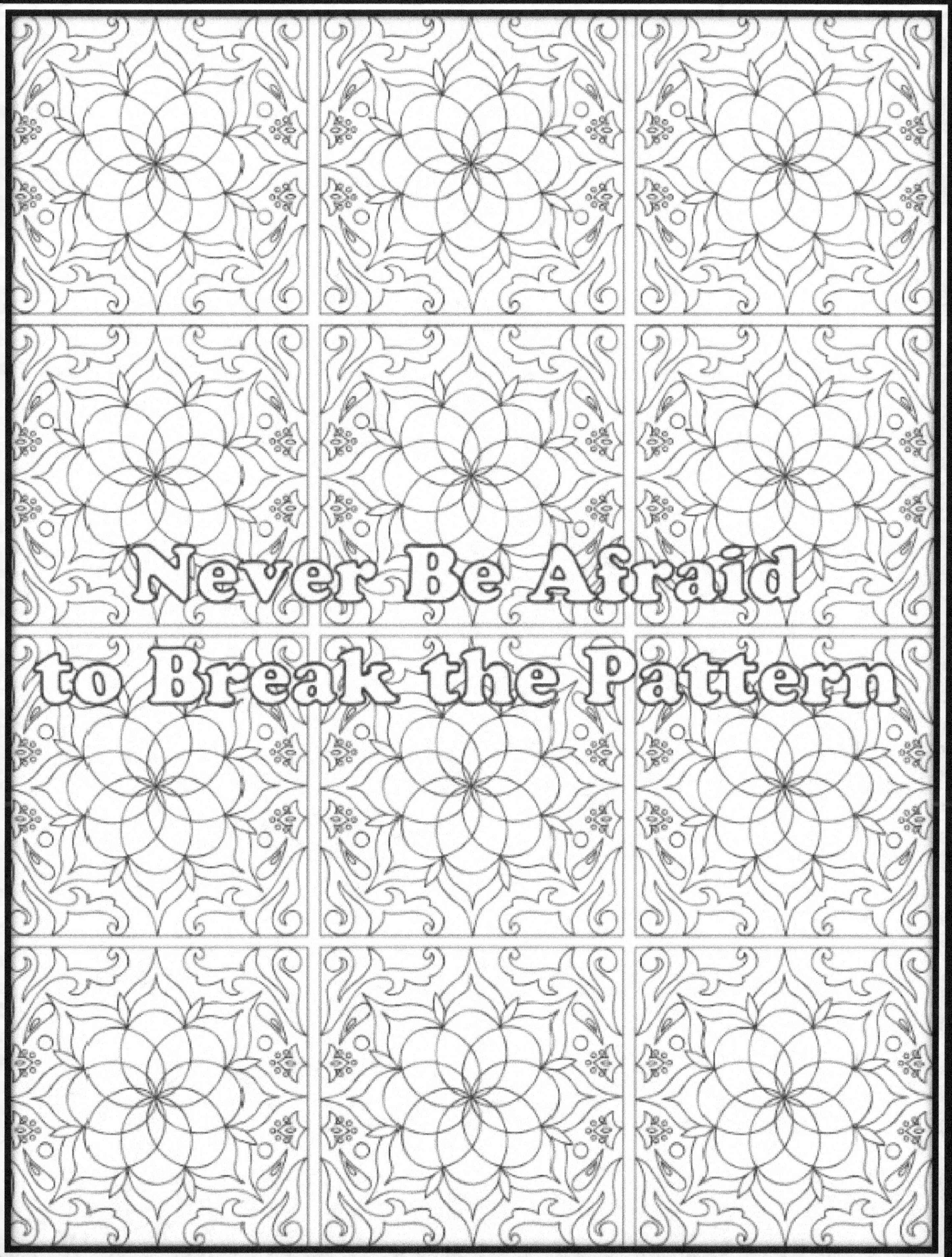

Never Be Afraid
to Break the Pattern

PEACE

Knowledge is Knowing
that a Tomato is a Fruit.
Wisdom is Knowing
it Does Not Belong
in a Fruit Salad

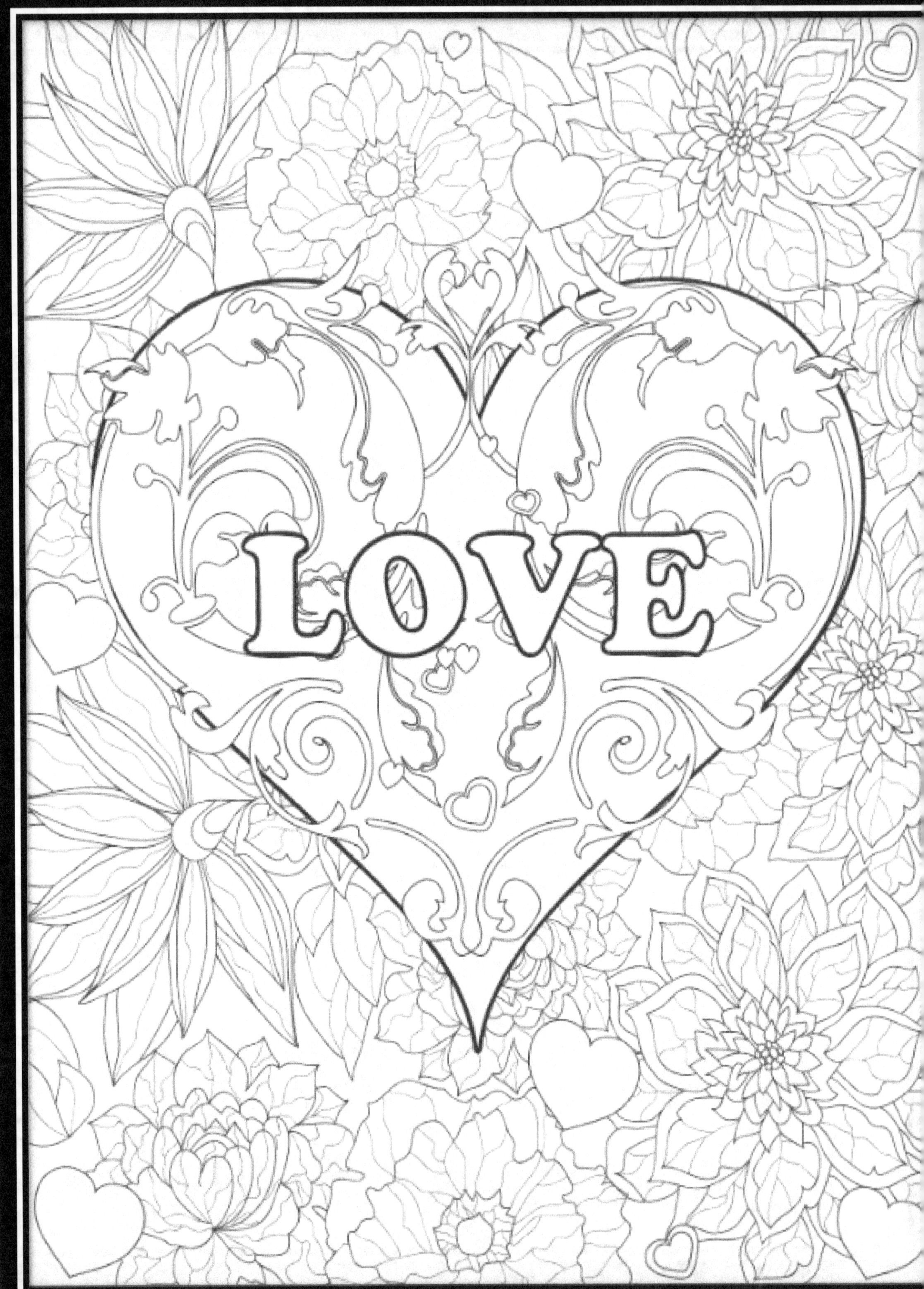

LOVE

Fierce

If You Want to Fly,
Give Up Everything
That Weighs You Down.

DREAM

INSPIRATION

GODDESS

GRATITUDE

CONQUERER

SUCCESSFUL

KARMA.
It's the Circle of Life.

Every FLOWER is a
SOUL BLOSSOMING in Nature.

Friends
are the Family
we choose for
ourselves

www.ingramcontent.com/pod-product-compliance
Lightning Source LLC
Chambersburg PA
CBHW081635250726
48657CB00009B/2891